COOKING

with a jersey girl

COOKING

with a jersey girl

Joyce Ann Staples

TATE PUBLISHING *& Enterprises*

Published by Tate Publishing & Enterprises, LLC
127 E. Trade Center Terrace | Mustang, Oklahoma 73064 USA
1.888.361.9473 | www.tatepublishing.com

Tate Publishing is committed to excellence in the publishing industry. The company reflects the philosophy established by the founders, based on Psalm 68:11,
"The Lord gave the word and great was the company of those who published it."

Book design copyright © 2007 by Tate Publishing, LLC. All rights reserved.
Cover design by Lindsay B. Behrens
Interior design by Kandi Evans

Published in the United States of America

ISBN: 978-1-60462-497-7
1. Cooking: Regional
2. Italian
07.11.05

Table of
CONTENTS

INTRODUCTION

I am neither a trained chef nor a professional cook. I don't own a restaurant, a gourmet food store, nor am I a caterer; although, I come from a family of restaurant owners. But my credentials are simply this: I am a Jersey girl through and through with 100% Italian roots in Central New Jersey. I live not far from where I grew up with my family; my parents; three brothers; all eight uncles on my mother's side; my aunt, uncle, and two cousins next door on my father's side; twenty or thirty cousins within walking distance; several great aunts and uncles; *and* great Italian grocery stores. Also, within walking distance.

You could say that I was raised in my grandmother's kitchen, watching her cook and bake as if it were magic. How well I know now that it certainly was not magic. Coming from a big Italian family, I'm not much different than most second-generation Italian Americans born and raised right here in New Jersey. I have learned about Italian foods and customs from my family. Still to this day, I will ask my mother about a certain dish that my grandmother and my zias (aunts), Carmela and Florence, would make. And, thank God, my father made me taste everything—well, almost everything. I drew the line at *some* things.

I love the Italian pronunciation of some of the dishes. I usually butcher the Italian words. If my grandmother heard me, she would not be happy, and I can picture her standing in front of me—all five feet of her—shaking her finger at me saying, "The day will come, my JoyceAnn, when you will wish you had learned to speak Italian." Truer words have never been spoken. But I never have, and that's a shame. Only a few words did I learn to pronounce with such flair . . . but not to be discussed here.

My grandmother, aunts, and mother spent many hours preparing those delicious meals. How well I remember Sunday sauce. They started cooking their pot of sauce on Saturday morning, allowing it to simmer all day, refrigerated it overnight, then continued again Sunday morning. Sunday was the day for a big family meal. Breakfast consisted of fried meatballs, crispy Italian bread, and the aroma of wonderful coffee perking on the stove, and *demitasse*. How I loved my grandmother's *demitasse* sets, and she was very proud of them also. It was not necessary to be in the house to enjoy these fabulous smells, that aroma floated through the air, and just approaching the driveway was all that was necessary. The aroma of the tomato sauce still simmering, meatballs frying, and fresh homemade baked treats—usually a custard-filled sponge cake or my grandmother's claim to fame, tomato soup cake. The house was usually filled with company and food; what could be better? And, my grandmother always made homemade "macaroni" for Sunday dinner.

I can't tell you exactly when, but I found myself enjoying every aspect of preparing the dishes I loved as a child, creating some of my own and discussing and sharing recipes with others. I think the person most surprised by my culinary creativity in the kitchen was my mother. Until that point, I depended on her to make everything. Many times, I still do. But soon I discovered I had a talent for cooking and experimenting with new and different flavors. As my love for cooking grew and my skills improved, and with slight variations to the original recipes, I could cut down on the calories, fats, and sugars and spend less time preparing. I'm turned off when a recipe has more than eight ingredients. When prep time is longer than thirty minutes. When you can't find the necessary items in your local food store and need to order online. I like simple recipes that I can either dress-up or down, revise if I feel like having something different today. Also, I believe in fewer calories, which does not mean sacrificing flavor. Most recipes can be revised, and no one, honestly, no one will notice the difference.

Every recipe has a story, and I love telling them. I am

inspired by the people around me. Sometimes I get an urge to jump into the kitchen after watching a movie on television, such as *Like Water for Chocolate*, *Big Night*, *Chocolat*, or *Under the Tuscan Sun*. After watching *Big Night*, the next day I made stuffed artichokes; after *Chocolat*, I made truffles; and after watching *Under the Tuscan Sun,* I wanted to be her, but instead I made poached pears. And, after watching *Like Water for Chocolate*, I realized something very important—that what my grandmother, aunts, and mother did was for their families. Nothing was stronger than family. They cooked with passion and love. Every dish they placed on the table was served with pride and from the heart. My purpose in telling these stories is that I feel all this will be gone with my generation. My daughters do not have the memories I have of their great grandparents, and certainly not future generations. I doubt they realize how much of an impression family has made on all of us. This is a testimony to the memory of all of our grandparents and relatives who brought so much to this country and still enrich our lives to this day. I feel I keep their memory alive in every recipe, every story, and every delicious bite.

Which brings me full circle to why I want to share these recipes, tips, and stories. I love cooking because I have always been around it. No one should feel as if they are slaving over the stove or that it's a chore. A little ingenuity, today's conveniences, and fabulous food stores make it easier and fun, and cutting back on time and calories makes every bite so much better.

Try these recipes and I hope you find, as I did, how easy it is to cook with flare, create your personal style, and most importantly, *enjoy*!

FRITTATAS & EGGS

I love frittatas, the Italian word for omelets. The possibilities are endless. They are low in calories and quick and simple to make. At one time when Fridays were meatless, frittatas and egg dishes were great Friday night dinners. Sometimes my grandmother would make a frittata for lunch, serve it with a large tossed salad, a vegetable, and some fresh Italian bread from the bakery around the corner. It was the big meal for that day. You can be as creative as you want. Some of my best frittatas have come about from quick, last-minute thinking. Add some leftover vegetables, slices of Jersey tomatoes or even potatoes.

The first time I made a frittata, I had a little difficulty getting the technique just right. A little practice, and I mastered it. I recommend spraying your skillet with a non-stick spray and using olive oil to give it that nice Italian flavor.

I have included five frittatas and two egg dishes, which are my favorites. I think once you try them, they will become a favorite of yours also.

Asparagus Frittata

This is my mother's version, and I have not revised it. I love serving this dish with a chilled salad of spring mix greens and grape tomatoes tossed lightly with oil and wine vinegar. I also like this served cold over salad greens for lunch. Enjoy!

10-12 large fresh eggs
¼ cup water
1 bunch asparagus, hard ends cut off
Olive oil
Fresh-grated parmesan or Romano cheese
Salt and pepper to taste

Cover asparagus with plastic wrap and microwave until tender, about 9 minutes. Cool slightly and cut into 1-inch pieces. Break all the eggs into a large mixing bowl. Add the water and beat well with a fork or whisk. Heat olive oil in a 12 or 13-inch skillet until almost hot.

Turn on the broiler. Place asparagus in pan and stir to mix well so that all asparagus is coated with oil. Pour egg mixture on top of asparagus. Sprinkle with salt and pepper.

Tip the pan from side to side so the liquid runs under and starts to cook. Run a rubber spatula around the sides of the pan at the same time to prevent burning. Do this until most of the mixture has been absorbed. Lower heat to medium. Continue to run the spatula around the edges, lifting as much of the frittata as possible. Sprinkle parmesan cheese on top and place under broiler until puffy and lightly browned. Slide frittata onto a serving plate. Serve immediately, or refrigerate and reheat in microwave to serve later.

Fried Spaghetti Frittata

This was a dish my grandmother made for Wednesday's dinner. Wednesday was a meatless day in my grandparent's home because of a story my grandfather told us about when he was a boy. It seems on a Wednesday afternoon he was walking across a bridge of railroad tracks when he suddenly realized a train was coming. There was nowhere to go, and he could not outrun the train, so he climbed down and held on for dear life while the train passed above him. While he was holding on and hanging from the bridge, he prayed to God that if he was saved, he would never eat meat again on Wednesdays. Hence, meatless Wednesdays.

1 pound spaghetti, cooked al dente and drained well
8–10 large eggs
1 tablespoon Italian seasoning
1 tablespoon garlic powder
2 tablespoons pinoli nuts, toasted
Olive oil, to cover bottom of large skillet

**½ cup grated parmesan or Romano cheese,
reserve some for garnish
Salt and pepper to taste**

Place pinoli nuts in large skillet on high heat and cook approximately 3–5 minutes, until aromatic. Pour enough oil in skillet over nuts to coat bottom. Heat oil until almost hot but not smoking. Break eggs into large mixing bowl. Add salt, pepper, and seasonings. Beat eggs with fork. Add spaghetti to egg mixture. Toss well. Pour mixture over pinoli nuts in skillet on medium heat. Allow to set slightly. Turn on broiler and place under broiler until lightly browned. Sprinkle with grated cheese. Cut into wedges and serve warm.

Frittata Biscotti

Not exactly what you're thinking, but close. My mother gets the credit for this one! Crackers and eggs and you will be surprised at how amazing and tasty this frittata is. The entire flavor comes from the cheeses and seasonings. Uneeda Biscuits were originally used but you may use any cracker. Try a cheese-flavored cracker!

6-8 eggs, well beaten
¼ teaspoon salt
¼ teaspoon pepper
¼ teaspoon crushed red pepper flakes
½ cup grated parmesan and/or Romano cheese
(You can also substitute cheddar.)
6-8 plain white crackers (saltines, Uneeda
Biscuits, or water crackers)
Cooking spray
¼ cup olive oil
Salt and pepper to taste
Extra cheese for topping

Spray large skillet with cooking spray and heat the olive oil to medium. Beat eggs in large bowl, adding the salt, pepper, red pepper flakes, and cheese. Pour into skillet, swirling from side to side. Over top of the skillet, crush the crackers into approximately 2-inch pieces. Drop into mixture and finish cooking frittata by lightly browning both sides, either on the stove or by placing under the broiler. Sprinkle extra cheese on top just before serving. Add salt and pepper to taste and serve warm.

Onion and Cheddar Frittata

I was looking to make something different, and my taste buds were calling for sweet but tangy. I checked the refrigerator to see what I had handy and remembered I had a package of cheddar cheese. I added the onions as an afterthought and came up with this fabulous tasting frittata. It is so delicious because the onions give it a nice sweet taste, while the cheddar gives it enough bite and saltiness. Unlike its counterpart, the asparagus frittata, I like to serve this warm over slightly heated salad greens tossed lightly with vinaigrette.

1 medium Spanish onion, sliced into rings
10–12 large eggs
¼ cup water
½ teaspoon crushed red pepper flakes
½ teaspoon Italian seasoning
½ cup shredded sharp cheddar cheese
Non-stick cooking spray

Olive oil
Salt and pepper to taste

Spray large skillet with cooking spray. Pour in enough olive oil to coat bottom of pan. Place on medium to high heat. Slice the onion into rings and add to the skillet. Immediately stir to coat all the onions with the oil. Add the red pepper flakes and Italian seasoning. Stir well. Cook until onions are translucent and aromatic. In a medium bowl, beat eggs well, add water, and beat again. Pour eggs over onions in skillet. Immediately swirl mixture from side to side. With a cooking spatula, go around edges, making sure mixture does not stick. Continue this method for a few minutes until frittata is set on the bottom. Sprinkle the cheddar over the top of the frittata. Place skillet under heated broiler until cheese is melted and top of frittata is puffy and set, about 1 minute. There should be no liquid on top. Slide onto large serving plate. Add salt and pepper to taste. Serve warm.

Parmesan and Gruyere Mini Frittatas

I take full credit for these delicious mini frittatas. Feeling rather creative one evening, I decided to take a simple quiche recipe, and see just what I could do with it to reduce the calories, carbohydrates, and fat content. And this was the result. I brought them to the office and everyone raved. I also experimented by substituting crabmeat and lobster in place of the bacon. And needless to say, those were a hit too! Try my recipe for mini frittatas and watch them disappear before your eyes.

2 ounces grated parmesan cheese
4 ounces grated gruyere cheese
3 eggs, beaten
1 cup lite cream
¼ teaspoon nutmeg
½ pound bacon
1 muffin pan (12 muffins)

Place bacon in microwave covered with paper towel. Microwave on high about 7–9 minutes. Turn bacon over and microwave about 4 minutes, until crispy. While bacon is cooking, grate the gruyere and parmesan—set aside. Beat eggs with a fork, add cream, sprinkle with nutmeg, and stir. Spray muffin pan with cooking spray. When bacon has cooled, crumble into small pieces and place in bottom of muffin pan. Place about 2 tablespoons of the cheeses on top of bacon. Slowly pour egg mixture over cheeses, filling each tin half way. Place in 350 degree oven for 30–35 minutes. Turn pan to brown evenly. The mini frittatas are done when puffy, lightly browned and there is no liquid in the center.

Peppers and Eggs

Everyone knows this one. It must be a staple in Italian families. I ate pepper and egg sandwiches when other kids were eating peanut butter and jelly. I have never had a peanut butter and jelly sandwich in my life. Peanut butter went on crackers, and jelly went on toast. It's just the way it was in my family. But, I grew up with taste buds no other child had. I loved these sandwiches and still do today. I make this in omelet form for breakfast. It's hearty enough to hold me for several hours and at the same time not high in calories or fat and great for low-carb diets. You can make this for breakfast in minutes with my easy rendition of this classic Italian favorite. Of course, I enjoy it best with crispy Italian bread (there go the carbs).

6 large eggs
1 jar roasted red peppers or pepper salad
3–4 tablespoons grated parmesan cheese
Salt and pepper
Olive oil

Spray large frying pan with cooking spray. Add just enough olive oil to coat bottom of pan. Heat over medium. Break eggs into frying pan, one at a time, and allow to cook. Slice and chop the roasted red peppers and add to the eggs. With a fork, scramble the eggs and peppers together in the pan, breaking the yolks. Sprinkle with salt and pepper and some of the cheese. Allow to cook the same as scrambled eggs or an omelet. When the eggs start to brown slightly around the edges, flip the eggs and cook on the other side. Sprinkle with more of the parmesan cheese. Slide the eggs out of the pan onto a serving dish. Eat half and save the other half for later. Serve with Italian bread. Great any time of the year and any time of the day—breakfast, lunch, or a quick late-night supper. This is a delicious way to start or end your day.

Potatoes and Eggs

So easy to make and so delicious to eat. Although this dish is eggs, it is a hearty dish. I think of this as a winter lunch recipe. Fried potatoes and a sprinkling of crushed red pepper flakes, what could be tastier? Add a good quality olive oil, Italian bread and we're in heaven. My grandmother used the seeds from hot cherry peppers to season this dish; however, I believe in making life easy and not so hot, so I use the crushed red pepper flakes. If you like hot, use the peppers. If you want, you can eliminate the cherry peppers and crushed red pepper flakes. It's delicious either way.

3 baking potatoes, peeled and sliced
6 large eggs, beaten
1–2 teaspoons crushed red pepper flakes or 1–2 chopped hot cherry peppers
½ cup olive oil
Salt and pepper to taste
Fresh-grated parmesan cheese

Pour olive oil in a large, heavy skillet and heat for 1 minute on high. Add the slices of potatoes, cook for 1 minute on high. Reduce heat to medium and allow potatoes to fry until tender and slightly browned around the edges, approximately 15 minutes. At the same time, add the chopped hot cherry peppers or the red pepper flakes and continue cooking with the potatoes. In a medium bowl, scramble the eggs and sprinkle with salt and pepper. When potatoes are done, reduce heat to medium-low, pour eggs over top and allow to set. Flip eggs over when they are browning around the edges. Continue cooking 1 minute longer. Sprinkle with grated parmesan cheese and fresh-ground black pepper. Serve immediately.

Tomatoes and Eggs

This is definitely an old Italian favorite. Sometimes I call my mother and ask her to make it for me. It's easy and so very good. It is especially good on a chilly afternoon; however, I also enjoy it cold over whole wheat bread. Try it!

1 large can crushed tomatoes
8–10 eggs, beaten
Salt and pepper to taste
Olive oil

Spray a large frying pan with cooking spray. Pour about ¼ cup olive oil in bottom of pan and add the tomatoes. Season with salt and pepper. Cook for 15–20 minutes. Break eggs into a medium-sized bowl and beat well. Add beaten eggs to tomatoes in pan and mix with a fork. Continue to mix with fork, the same as you would for scrambled eggs. Allow cooking until softly set but eggs are cooked thoroughly and there is no liquid visible. You may place the entire frying pan under the broiler for about 1 minute. Spoon onto a serving plate and serve with crispy semolina or whole wheat Italian bread. Delicious!

SALADS

Salad is the staff of life for me. I love salads. I enjoy tossing different items in my salads and blending a mixture of flavors in my dressings. My grandmother always said that some things *always* go together and some things *never* go together. She made the most delicious tomato salad with, of course, Jersey tomatoes, but she never put vinegar in her tomato salad. That was a definite no-no! She *always* used oregano on her salads, but *never* in her sauce. She would always use good quality olive oil, fresh garlic cloves, and fabulously sweet-tasting onions. And I follow her rule today. However, I love today's flavored vinegars and I use them in my green salads, but *never* in my tomato salad. My grandmother also made a dandelion salad that looked like a picture. The color green of the dandelion stems glistened from the olive oil dressing together with the little speckles of white from the chopped garlic. However, I could never bring myself to taste the dandelion salad. I think it was simply that I thought of it as eating grass or weeds. *But*, I make an arugula salad that looks and *tastes* as if it could compete with my grandmother's dandelion salad any day. Adding little touches here and there of different items, such as grape tomatoes, chickpeas, garden green peas or beans, mandarin oranges, or fresh orange sections, slices of fresh vegetables, seasonings and herbs. And don't forget the dressing. Something as simple as olive oil and wine vinegar, or try an infused vinegar. Drizzle over the top, add fresh-ground black pepper, a dash of oregano and *bravo*—a great-tasting salad that your family and friends will devour.

Arugula Salad

For a change of pace, try arugula instead of lettuce. Warming the arugula just slightly gives it a different flavor twist against the cold of the other ingredients. The flavors meld together, and your taste buds will jump for joy. Make a semisweet dressing or simple olive oil and wine vinegar with just a little sugar. The sweetness goes nicely with the taste of the arugula. It is just a little different. Serve with crispy bread or place a few large croutons on top.

1 bunch arugula, washed and drained
Pinch of salt
½ carton grape tomatoes
1 can mandarin oranges, chilled and drained
4 or 5 slices of each Spanish and red onions
4 tablespoons olive oil for sauté pan
4 or 5 tablespoons olive oil for dressing
2 tablespoons balsamic vinegar
Fresh-ground black pepper
1 teaspoon Italian seasoning

1 packet sugar substitute
Salt and pepper to taste

In a small bowl, place olive oil, vinegar, Italian seasoning, sugar substitute and whisk briskly. Set aside. After washing arugula, drain well by pressing out excess water with paper towels. Add oil to sauté pan, place arugula in pan and sprinkle with salt and pepper. Turn with tongs until just wilted and heated through. Place in a mixing bowl. Spoon on the dressing, tossing gently and mix with the tongs. Add the cold tomatoes, onions, and the orange sections. Give it another twist of fresh black pepper. The greens will glisten. Serve warmed or chilled.

Chickpea Salad

Cece Salad

My grandmother used chickpeas in salads and pasta dishes. I like the flavor and crunchiness. I make a delicious salad with just the chickpeas and a few seasonings. It's a great chilled side dish for hot summer days or anytime you want something fast. Fresh parsley is the secret ingredient in this dish and lots of it.

- 1 large can chickpeas
- 1 Bermuda onion, chopped
- 1 tablespoon dry parsley
- 1 tablespoon Italian seasoning
- ½ cup fresh parsley, chopped
- ½ cup olive oil
- Salt and pepper to taste

Drain the chickpeas and add to a medium-sized bowl. Sprinkle lightly with salt. Add fresh-ground black pepper. Add onion, dry parsley, fresh parsley, and Italian seasoning. Toss with the olive oil and refrigerate. Serve chilled.

Cucumber Salad with Sweet Dill Dressing

Salads are great for in between meals as those snacks we should have instead of the cookies and M&M's. I always have a bowl of salad in the refrigerator, and this cucumber salad is great for picking when those cravings hit. It's cool, sweet, crunchy, and healthy. The dressing can be used over salad greens or as a dipping sauce for other recipes. Enjoy!

2 firm cucumbers, peeled and sliced
1 medium Bermuda onion, chopped
Dressing:
1 cup light mayo
1 packet sugar substitute
1 tablespoon dry dill weed
1 tablespoon Italian seasoning
¼ cup honey mustard
Salt and pepper to taste

Place cucumbers and onion in a medium-sized bowl. In a jar fitted with a screw-on cap, add the mayo and the rest of the seasonings. Place the cap on the jar and shake vigorously until all ingredients are mixed. Pour over cucumbers and toss. Serve chilled. Refrigerate any leftover dressing.

Italian Style German Potato Salad

The credit for this recipe goes to my mother. Any potato will do, but my mother prefers little red new potatoes, and I prefer pancetta, although my mother always used bacon. Growing up, this was the *only* potato salad I ever had. I didn't know about potato salad with mayonnaise until my Uncle Butchy married Barbara Suhan (first generation Hungarian-American). I was about seven or eight years old. Affectionately known as Aunt Bobbie still to this day, she introduced potato and macaroni salad to our family. My grandmother said she never cared for the taste of mayonnaise, but I believe she just wasn't about to give credit to her new "non-Italian" daughter-in-law. By the way, Aunt Bobbie was the face of the telephone operator on the phone directory that year.

10 or 12 new red potatoes
½ pound bacon
1 medium Bermuda onion, chopped
Olive oil

½ teaspoon Italian seasoning
¼ teaspoon rosemary
Salt and pepper to taste

Wash potatoes and place in deep pot with enough water to cover potatoes. Sprinkle water with salt. Allow potatoes to cook until they are fork tender, not too soft, about 20 minutes. While potatoes are cooking, fry pancetta or bacon until crispy. Remove from pan and set aside. Do not rinse or wipe pan. Return pan to stove and on medium to high heat cook onion slices in the drippings. Add olive oil if needed. Cook onions until caramelized. Add the pancetta or bacon back into the frying pan with the onions and heat through. Remove from heat. When potatoes are ready, run cold water into the pot to slightly cool. Drain off water. When potatoes are still warm but cool enough to handle, slice each potato in half and place in a large bowl. Sprinkle with Italian seasoning, rosemary, salt, and pepper. Add the pancetta or bacon mixture and toss gently but well. Sprinkle with a dash of rosemary on top. Serve warm, cold, or room temperature.

Spring Mix Salad

Jersey Tomatoes, Toasted Pinoli Nuts, and Shaved Parmesan

If Caesar salad is "the king" of salads, then this is "the Queen." My creation, and I love it. I truly love salads! They are refreshing and light. With a little creativity, a salad can also be a main dish by adding chicken, slices of London broil, pasta, and my favorite, vegetables. I would imagine that most people prefer their salads cold. However, a different take on this great old standby would be to warm the salad greens just slightly. Either way, *this* salad is delightful and absolutely scrumptious! It's prepared in minutes, but you will savor its taste long after. Fresh Jersey tomatoes add a wonderful flavor, toasted pinoli nuts add crunch, but the shaved parmesan will get the standing ovation. Use a fresh wedge of parmesan cheese, high quality olive oil, and good balsamic vinegar. Everyone will ask for this recipe.

1 bag spring mix or 4 cups of any salad greens
1 small Bermuda onion, sliced in rings
4 or 5 radishes, sliced

2 Jersey picked tomatoes, quartered, or 1 pint of
cherry tomatoes from the vine
2 cucumbers, sliced
½ bottle Pinoli nuts or about 10unce toasted
1 teaspoon salt
Fresh-ground black pepper to taste
Dressing:
¼ cup olive oil
4 tablespoons balsamic vinegar
1 teaspoon oregano
1 teaspoon dry basil
1 teaspoon Italian seasoning
Parmesan shavings

Wash salad greens and drain. Dry with paper towels and place
in large platter or bowl. Add all other ingredients, except Pinoli
nuts. Set aside. In a small bowl, whisk together the olive oil,
vinegar, oregano, basil, and Italian seasoning. Set aside. In a
small sauté pan, over high heat, cook Pinoli nuts until lightly
brown, 2–3 minutes. Place the pinolis into the dressing and
stir. Pour the dressing gently over the salad and toss lightly. I
like to add additional black pepper. With a vegetable peeler,
shave parmesan cheese curls onto the salad, about 10–12 curls.
Toss lightly with tongs. Serve either as a side dish with din-

ner or make it your main course by adding cooked shrimp, chicken, beef, or leftover vegetables!

Tomato Soup Macaroni Salad

Several years ago, a dear friend lost her battle with cancer. This recipe is in her memory.

The first time Carol told me of her tomato soup macaroni salad, I made a face, shook my head, and told her *no thank you*. She made me try it, and I was hooked. It became a favorite and a nice variation from regular pasta salads.

    1 pound pasta shells
    1 can tomato soup, do not rinse, save the can
    ½ can white vinegar
    ½ can olive oil
    1 cucumber, diced
    1 small onion, diced
    1 small jar pimentos, diced

Cook pasta al dente. Rinse with cold water and drain well. Cool pasta. Pour tomato soup over pasta and toss. Slice cucumber and onion and add to pasta. Add the pimentos and toss. Fill the empty tomato soup can with half olive oil and half white vinegar. Add to pasta. Toss well. Refrigerate and serve chilled.

VEGETABLES

My grandmother prepared vegetables in the most delicious ways. I honestly cannot say that as a child I savored these dishes; however, today I love them. I sauté broccoli, spinach, broccoli rabe, escarole, cauliflower, and cabbage. I love the taste of the vegetables tossed with olive oil, garlic, and onions. The method for preparing each one is similar. Broccoli can either be fresh or frozen spears. It does not affect the taste. I prefer frozen broccoli because there is less waste, and it's easier. Spinach I like fresh. Baby spinach does not have the thick stems and is really tasty and especially good in salads. Broccoli rabe is usually bitter and should be boiled first until very tender and the bitterness removed. I also boil escarole. Cabbage is as easy as slicing and frying, with lots of onions. Cauliflower is the reigning queen, as far as I'm concerned. I microwave it first, then sauté it with lots of onions. And green beans marinara, or as my grandmother called it "string bean stew." For all of these vegetables, use a good quality olive oil, lots of onions, fresh garlic, and crushed red pepper flakes. Don't forget the fresh-grated cheese and fresh-ground black pepper.

Asparagus with Lemon and Garlic

This is my favorite way to serve this delectable vegetable. I always think of spring when I see asparagus, but of course now it can be purchased all year. This recipe is easy and only takes minutes to prepare.

1 bunch asparagus
Salt and fresh-ground black pepper
3–4 garlic cloves, chopped
Olive oil
½ fresh lemon

Rinse asparagus under cold water. Place on microwaveable plate. Sprinkle with salt and pepper. Chop garlic into small pieces and add to asparagus. Cover with plastic wrap and microwave approximately 6–8 minutes. Check asparagus for tenderness and microwave approximately 2–3 minutes longer if needed. Remove from microwave, and squeeze lemon juice onto the asparagus. If you prefer to serve this dish cold, as I do, after adding the lemon, simply chill in the refrigerator for a few hours or overnight. The lemon adds just enough tang. This is a great side dish with seafood, especially during the warm days of summer. I garnish with a lemon wedge on the side of the plate. It's pretty and quite refreshing, besides tasty.

Cauliflower with Caramelized Onions

My mother makes this dish often. It is truly a family favorite and one need not be a vegetable lover. The sweetness of the sautéed Spanish onions gives the cauliflower a terrific flavor. Add plenty of garlic, crushed red pepper flakes, and always add the stems and leaves of the cauliflower, they add a great deal of taste.

    1 medium to large head of cauliflower
    2 large Spanish onions, cut in to medium wedges
    ¾ cup olive oil
    ½ teaspoon crushed red pepper flakes
    2 teaspoons fresh parsley or 1 teaspoon dry
    parsley flakes
    5–6 garlic cloves, chopped
    Salt and pepper

Cut cauliflower into wedges, place on plate, and cover with

plastic wrap. Microwave for 5 minutes. Heat oil in pan, add onions, and cook until translucent. Add cauliflower, red pepper flakes, parsley, garlic, salt, and pepper. Continue cooking approximately 5 minutes, or until cauliflower starts to brown. Add more oil if needed. Add a pinch (maybe two) of crushed red pepper flakes. Serve hot or cold.

Frank's Eggplant Parmesan

One day while sitting in the office on a quiet Saturday morning, Frank and I were discussing—what else?—food. I mentioned that eggplant parmesan is my very favorite. Frank said he had the best recipe for eggplant parmesan, and that the secret is Swiss cheese together with mozzarella. I simply had to try this. I can honestly tell you that he was absolutely right. The taste was amazing: cheesy, tangy, and yet so Italian. You will devour it.

1–2 firm eggplants, peeled and sliced lengthwise
2 cups seasoned breadcrumbs
4 eggs, beaten
½ cup milk
1 cup grated parmesan or Romano cheese
2 teaspoons Italian seasoning
1 teaspoon garlic powder
1 teaspoon onion powder

Salt and pepper to taste
1 cup olive oil
1 pound Swiss cheese, thinly sliced
1 pound mozzarella, shredded or thinly sliced
2 cups grated parmesan or Romano cheese
1–2 quarts marinara sauce

Heat oil in large skillet. Beat eggs and milk together, add cheese. To breadcrumbs, add dry seasonings, salt, and pepper. Dip eggplant slices in egg mixture, then into breadcrumbs, placing them carefully (a few at a time) into the hot oil. Fry until golden on both sides and tender. Drain on paper towels. When all eggplant has been cooked, start assembling by spooning a ladle of sauce into bottom of 13x9 baking pan. Place first layer of eggplant on the sauce. Sprinkle with a handful of mozzarella, a handful of grated cheese, and a single layer of Swiss cheese. Spoon sauce over top and start the layering again until all the eggplant has been used. Top with Swiss cheese and sauce. Bake for 1 hour at 325 degrees or until bubbly and hot. Cool for 10 minutes before serving.

Greens and Beans

Escarole With White Kidney Beans

This is what I call soul food, and my grandmother would agree. It is definitely good for the soul, healthy for your body, and easy to make. The taste is absolutely delicious. My grandmother would bring home bags of escarole, then fill the kitchen sink with cold water, and rinse each leaf by hand, then re-rinse in cold water again by letting the leaves float in the sink until she was ready for them. I wash the leaves under running water for several minutes in a colander before boiling. Escarole will cook down to almost a quarter of what it starts at, so make sure you purchase enough. A good barometer is that 1 bunch of escarole is enough for 2 servings. My grandmother called this "greens and beans." I never knew it as escarole, but I knew the aroma and the taste. For a slightly spicier palate, add slices of pepperoni to this dish. What a tasty sensation! I love it either way.

1 or 2 heads escarole, washed well
Large stock pot filled with salted water

1 or 2 cans kidney beans (Do not drain.)
½ teaspoon crushed red pepper flakes
3–4 garlic cloves, chopped
Olive oil

Boil escarole until tender. Drain well, reserving about ½ cup of the cooking water. When slightly cooled, squeeze excess water out. In a large sauté pan, heat olive oil and add garlic. Add escarole and sauté until all escarole is a tender and thoroughly coated with the olive oil, but do not let the garlic brown. Add some of the pasta water. When the escarole is heated through, add the kidney beans and stir gently. Sprinkle the crushed red pepper flakes on top and serve steaming hot.

Hint: Do not add water to the canned beans. The water will foam from the residue in the cans.

Green Beans Marinara

My grandmother called this green bean stew. She made it every Monday from the sauce and meatballs that were left-over from Sunday's dinner. With the addition of a few cut-up potatoes, it became stew. Certainly you could add meatballs or stew meat; however, I prefer my green beans strew vegetarian style. And, on the few occasions that I do add potatoes, canned whole potatoes sliced in half are perfect. It saves time in the kitchen at the stove. I don't know anyone who isn't in favor of that.

1 pound fresh green beans, washed and tips removed

12–16 ounces marinara sauce

$1/$ cup olive oil

Salt and pepper

$1/4$ teaspoon crushed red pepper flakes

$1/3$ cup grated Italian cheese

1 16-ounce can whole potatoes (optional)

Place green beans in approximately 2 quarts of salted, boiling water. Cover and boil for about 10 minutes, checking the water level, and cook until desired tenderness. Heat marinara sauce, adding the crushed red pepper flakes. If you are adding potatoes, place them in the sauce to heat through. Drain green beans, reserving about 6 to 8 ounces of the water. Place green beans in serving bowl and add olive oil. Toss lightly. Add reserved water to the sauce and stir gently. When the sauce starts to bubble, pour over green beans. Toss gently, add grated cheese and fresh black pepper. Serve immediately.

Sautéed Broccoli and Shrimp

I have always loved sautéed broccoli by itself. One day, having lunch at LaFontana Ristaurante in the heart of downtown New Brunswick, I saw this on the menu and ordered it. Needless to say, I loved it. I have been making it ever since. In fact, I usually make extra because my daughter, Stephanie, enjoys it also.

1 16–20-ounce box frozen broccoli spears, defrosted
½ pound (about 10) cooked jumbo shrimp, tails removed
½ cup olive oil
5 or 6 cloves garlic, chopped
1 teaspoon crushed red pepper flakes
½ cup fresh-grated parmesan cheese
Salt and fresh-ground black pepper to taste
Lemon wedges

Place broccoli spears in medium hot oil. Allow to cook until browned on one side before turning. Add chopped garlic, red pepper flakes, salt, and pepper. Cook until lightly browned and the aroma of the garlic fills the air. Add the cooked shrimp and toss lightly. Continue cooking just until shrimp are heated through. Sprinkle with parmesan cheese and cook for 1 minute more. Allow cheese to fry slightly and get crispy. Place on serving dish. Sprinkle with a little more grated cheese, and add fresh-ground black pepper and lemon wedges.

Also, this dish is delicious by itself. You can prepare this recipe without the shrimp using the same ingredients and amounts as above.

Sauteed Spinach

This is definitely the easiest and one of the tastiest ways to serve this deliciously dark green vegetable. I have found sautéed spinach sold in Italian gourmet stores in my area and most Italian restaurants. My mother always referred to this dish as "peasant food" because it was grown in victory gardens across New Jersey during the 1930s. Besides the fact that it is good for you, sautéed spinach is easy to prepare and truly delicious. Serve with crispy Italian bread that you dip into the oil.

1 10-ounce bag of spinach
5–6 garlic cloves, crushed and chopped
Crushed red pepper flakes
Salt and pepper
⅓ cup olive oil

In a medium sauté pan sprayed with cooking spray, heat olive oil to medium hot. Wash the spinach and trim off the thick stems. Place in the oil and sauté for 1–2 minutes. Add the garlic and continue to sauté. Add the crushed red pepper and sauté for 5 minutes. Add salt and pepper to taste. Serve warm or cold.

Stuffed Artichokes

My mother made steamed artichokes that were outrageously delicious. Artichokes were one of her favorite dishes; I decided one year for Mother's Day to surprise my mother by making stuffed artichokes. I found an old recipe that belonged to my grandmother. Although I revised it slightly, I followed the basic recipe. My stuffed artichokes are incredible. I use a lot of stuffing and cook them until very tender. I believe the fabulous flavor comes from steaming over low heat for several hours, fresh herbs, and fresh-grated parmesan and Romano cheeses.

    5 or 6 large, firm artichokes or 9-12 baby
    artichokes
    3 cups Italian breadcrumbs
    2-3 handfuls grated parmesan and Romano
    cheeses mixed together
    1 whole garlic bulb, chopped
    3 tablespoons fresh parsley, chopped
    3 tablespoons fresh basil, chopped
    2 tablespoons Italian seasoning

Salt and pepper to taste
½ cup olive oil

Wash artichokes and shake out excess water. Cut stems from artichokes so they stand flat. With scissors, cut off thorny tips. Tap artichokes on counter to open slightly. Set aside. Chop garlic, parsley, and basil. Set aside. In a medium bowl add bread crumbs, grated cheeses, fresh herbs, salt, and pepper. Mix well. Holding an artichoke over the bowl of breadcrumbs, spoon the breadcrumb mixture between the leaves and stuff the center of each artichoke. Place each artichoke standing up, sides touching in a large pot with about 1 inch of water. Over top of each artichoke, drizzle olive oil just to moisten. Cover and steam on low for about 4 or 5 hours, replacing water as it evaporates. Serve warm or prepare a day or two ahead and then heat on the stove over very low heat or in the microwave,

Stuffed Peppers

This recipe is as easy to make as it is delicious to eat. If you like stuffed peppers, or if you do as my daughters always did and just eat the filling, I guarantee this recipe will have your family and friends devouring every morsel. My grandmother cooked her stuffed peppers in a pot of sauce. The peppers were stuffed with a beef, pork, and veal mixture similar to meatballs. I usually make my stuffed peppers vegetarian style. I believe in making life simple. Start with a box of flavored instant rice mix. I use rice pilaf, also, red and yellow bell peppers because they are sweeter tasting. If you choose to make this a heartier meal, then brown some meatloaf mix (beef, pork, and veal) or all beef and add to the cooked rice. You will love the sweetness of the peppers, the pungent flavors from the rice mix, and only a few minutes of preparation. Serve as a side dish or main meal. I guarantee there will be none left over, and if there is—*lunch*!

4 or 5 red bell peppers
1 box rice pilaf mix

Non-stick cooking spray
Olive oil

Wash peppers and slice off tops. Remove seeds from inside peppers and rinse again. Set aside. In a large skillet, prepare rice mix according to package directions. Preheat oven to 350 degrees. Spoon rice mixture into peppers, filling each pepper to the top. Spray shallow baking pan with non-stick cooking spray. Place peppers standing in pan. Drizzle 1 tablespoon of olive oil over each pepper or brush olive oil over entire pepper. Cover with foil and bake 45 minutes to 1 hour. Remove foil, turn off oven, and leave in about 15 minutes longer, just to brown slightly. Slice each pepper in half and serve warm.

Stuffed Portobello Caps

I was in the mood for something savory but light and felt rather creative. I had forgotten that a few days before, I purchased 6 large Portobello mushrooms (each one was about 4 to 5 inches in diameter). I knew I had to use them before they spoiled, and for the price I paid I certainly was not going to waste them. Also, I really felt like doing something different with them. I suddenly felt totally inspired and created this wonderful recipe. It is easy and only takes a few minutes to prepare. The ingredient that makes the difference is the grated parmesan cheese and my favorite, Italian seasoning. These stuffed Portobello mushrooms are fit for a queen—or a Jersey girl!

5 or 6 large Portobello mushroom caps
1½ - 2 pounds lump crabmeat or lobster filling
2 cups stuffing mix
½ - ¾ cup grated parmesan cheese
1 teaspoon dill
1 teaspoon Italian seasoning
1 stick butter plus 5 or 6 pats

Juice from 1 lemon
Cooking spray

Clean Portobellos with damp paper towel, removing all dark residue. Spray large skillet with cooking spray and melt butter completely. Add crabmeat or lobster and sauté until fully cooked. Add stuffing mix and stir together. Add grated cheese. Cook for 1–2 minutes. Spoon into mushroom caps, mounding slightly. Squeeze lemon over top and place 1 pat of butter over each mushroom. Sprinkle with dill. Place in 300 degree oven for 30 minutes, or until heated through. Serve as an appetizer, lunch, or have two for dinner. Scrumptious!

If your Portobellos are large, they will look fabulous served whole; however, you can serve them cut into wedges. I like to serve them as a side dish with steak or London broil. For any meal, these go great. Also, for lunch with a tossed green salad dressed with a dill mayonnaise.

PASTA
Macaroni

An Italian Jersey girl without a pasta recipe? As somebody (not me) would say, *forgetaboutit*! And, by the way, "macaroni" is the word in my family. There are hundreds of ways to serve pasta (macaroni), and I have included a few of my favorites. Starting with an all-time favorite, beans and macaroni (pasta e' fagoli). Sauces surely make the difference in flavor; however, the right type of pasta for the sauce is just as important. My mother and grandmother were mavens when it came to putting together a quick marinara sauce, which they served over thin spaghetti #8. It had to be #8. My mother still insists on #8. In twenty minutes we were ready to sit down and eat. The aroma filled every room in the house.

Today, I love to create and blend different flavors. I toss gorgonzola cheese with penne. Another idea surfaced one day while I was at my local grocer checking out the various cheeses. I purchased a sun-dried tomato and pesto cheese combination that I prepared with bowties. That was truly delicious. The sauce dictates the size of the pasta. A marinara sauce poured over thin spaghetti is just perfect. A thick pesto goes nicely tossed with rigatoni. A hearty meat sauce goes perfectly with lasagna or baked pasta dishes. Be creative and use different cheeses and seasonings and you will discover a world of fabulous flavors. Fresh herbs are another way of adding or layering flavors to a simple red sauce. And don't be afraid to spice it up.

Baked Spaghetti Pie

My grandmother always prepared baked spaghetti pie for Easter. It was a spring tradition and one of my favorites then and certainly is now. However, I make this dish for Christmas. The first time I made it, my cousins raved about it and, of course, remembered my grandmother making it. My mother's first cousins (my second cousins) actually asked me for the recipe, and I could not have been more flattered.

For this recipe you need a large baking pan. The pan I use is a 21x13 stainless steel restaurant pan. I have used a 16x10 pan and cut the recipe in half. I always spray the pan well with cooking spray.

2 pounds Perciatelli, cooked according to package directions
18 large eggs, well beaten in a very large bowl
1 pound each Cappicolla, Genoa salami, and Pepperoni, cut into small pieces
1 pound mozzarella, cut into small cubes

1½ pounds Ricotta
2 bottles Pinoli nuts

Drain the Perrciatelli well. Add to the eggs and mix well. Add all other ingredients and again mix well. Pour into pan and cover with foil. Bake at 350 degrees for 45 minutes. Uncover and bake for 45 minutes more. Test by putting a knife through the center. If the knife comes out clean, it is baked. If it is not firm all the way through, place back in the oven and test every 10 minutes until firm. Remove from oven and cool in pan for about 15 minutes. When completely cooled, remove from pan and refrigerate. To serve warm, heat in microwave. Serve warm or cold.

Hint: I salt only the pasta water because the meats have plenty of salt. I mix the mixture with my hands to ensure all ingredients are well blended.

Beans and Macaroni

Pasta e' fagoli

This was a poverty dish in the 1930s. Today it is an epicurean delight. I honestly think that as an infant and toddler, I was fed beans and macaroni instead of baby food. In the 1970s, my uncles opened an Italian family-style restaurant in South Brunswick. The menu featured "pasta e' fagoli" as a lunch special. It went over so big that it became part of their everyday menu, and that was many years before Italian restaurants throughout Central New Jersey started to include this delicious dish on their menus. My grandmother served beans and macaroni as a soup, but as a main dish. Several years ago, an associate and I were hosting a lunch. I was to serve lunch, and he would serve dessert. I asked my mother if she would make the beans and macaroni; I would make an antipasti, and my aunt would make her lemon drop cookies. My mother was thrilled to show off her culinary talents; in fact, she made a point of telling me that she would also be there to serve it. And serve she did. The invitations stated the menu. We had a packed house. My mother and her delicious "pasta e' fagoli" were thrust into stardom. Everyone wanted the recipe and a few wanted to hire her to cook for them. And, not to be out-done, my aunt's lemon drop cookies were the co-stars. This recipe is easy and delicious.

> ½ pound elbow or ditalini pasta, cooked al dente and drained well
> 1 can white canelli beans (Do not drain.)
> 4–5 celery stalks, sliced thin
> 1 small onion, diced
> ½ teaspoon crushed red pepper flakes
> Salt and pepper to taste
> 1 32-ounce jar marinara sauce
> Olive oil

Reserve 1–2 cups of the pasta water. Pour olive oil in bottom of 4-quart sauce pot, just to coat. Sauté onion lightly. Add red pepper flakes and celery. Stir well until all is coated and celery has softened. Add marinara and ½ cup of the pasta water. Heat sauce until bubbly. Add cooked pasta to the pot, a little at a time. Stir gently. The pasta will soak up the sauce if you add it too quickly. Add some of the pasta water. Add the remainder of the pasta and the remainder of the water. Stir gently. Serve immediately. Crispy Italian bread is a must for dipping into that delicious broth. (I also sprinkle on additional red pepper flakes and black pepper.)

Linguini, Shrimp, and Peas

This is my daughter Stephanie's favorite pasta dish. It is easy to make and so delicious too. I use canned clam sauce for added flavor, frozen peas, and cooked shrimp. The secret to the flavor is in the fresh herbs and lots of fresh-grated cheese. Serve with garlic bread and a tossed salad.

    1 pound linguini, cooked al dente and drained
    well, reserve some pasta water
    ½ pound cooked shrimp, tails removed
    1 can white clam sauce
    ½ bag frozen peas (not petite)
    1 cup olive oil
    Fresh-grated parmesan cheese
    Salt and pepper to taste
    1–2 tablespoons fresh basil
    1–2 tablespoons fresh parsley
    4–5 garlic cloves, chopped

1 teaspoon crushed red pepper flakes
1 large lemon, cut into wedges

Pour the oil into a large frying pan. Sauté garlic, adding basil, parsley, salt, pepper, and crushed red pepper flakes. Stir so garlic does not brown. Add clam sauce and shrimp. Cook for 2 minutes, just until heated. Add peas and toss lightly. Remove from heat. Place pasta on a serving plate. Immediately sprinkle with grated cheese and toss. Pour the sauce with the shrimp and peas over the pasta. Toss lightly. Add some pasta water if needed. Add fresh-grated cheese on top. Sprinkle with chopped fresh basil and parsley for garnish.

Mrs. Marinucci's Manicotti

Mrs. Marinucci lived two blocks from our house. She gave this recipe to my mother more than forty years ago. I found it four years ago in an old recipe file and surprised everyone when I made the manicotti for a Sunday dinner. My mother came to my home early that day, and I was just about to start filling the manicotti. So, mother filled and I finished cooking (a real roll reversal). Everyone loved them. Homemade manicotti shells are thin, almost light-as-air pancakes filled with a mixture of ricotta and mozzarella cheeses seasoned with fresh parsley, salt, and pepper. Marinara sauce or a meat sauce that's not too chunky goes best. The shells can be made the day before and stored in the refrigerator. You will marvel at how thin and light the shells are. A delightful treat. This recipe makes about 16 shells.

Manicotti shells:
1 cup flour
½ cup water

½ cup milk
3 large eggs
½ teaspoon salt
Olive oil

Filling:
2 pounds whole milk or part skim ricotta
4 ounces whole milk or part skim mozzarella
½ cup fresh-grated parmesan
1 large egg, beaten
2 tablespoons fresh parsley, chopped
½ teaspoon salt
Fresh-ground black pepper
Non-stick cooking spray

Whisk together all ingredients for the shells, except the olive oil. Refrigerate about 20 to 30 minutes. Spray a small skillet with non-stick cooking spray. Pour just enough oil in bottom to coat evenly. Over medium heat, with a small ladle, pour batter into pan and immediately swirl from side to side to coat bottom of pan. Shells will cook in about 1 minute or less. With tongs, flip the shell over and cook for a few seconds longer. Remove from pan. Place wax paper between layers of shells, or, if not filling immediately, cover with foil or plastic wrap and refrigerate. Preheat oven to 350 degrees.

In a large bowl, place all ingredients for the filling and stir vigorously. Place a tablespoonful of filling into the center of each shell, then roll shells, seam side down. Place about ½ cup of sauce in the bottom of a baking pan that has been sprayed with non-stick cooking spray. Place the shells in the pan in a single layer, side by side. Pour sauce over top of shells. Sprinkle a good handful of grated cheese over the top. Place in oven and bake for 45 minutes, until sauce bubbles. Remove from oven and let sit for about 10 minutes before serving.

Penne, Pesto, Tomatoes, and Gorgonzola

We were having a birthday luncheon at the office for our boss, and a few of us were making different items. I decided I really wanted to show off, and knowing my boss loved pesto and pasta, I decided to make a pesto dish. I figured, why not combine and layer all my favorite flavors and then give it one big *wow* of flavor at the end? I used crumbled gorgonzola cheese for that last wow. Everyone loved it. I had never used gorgonzola in pasta before then. And, much to my surprise, they were eating it cold. So, it can be served either hot as a main dish or cold as a pasta salad. Either way, it was such a big hit! You can add cooked chicken slices also. When you make this, it will be your turn to show off and *wow* the crowd.

1 pound penne pasta, reserve about 1–1½ cups pasta water
½ cup pesto

1 16-ounce can petite tomatoes with olive oil
and garlic
4–5 garlic cloves, chopped
Fresh parsley, chopped
1 tablespoon fresh basil, chopped or 1 teaspoon
dry basil
Olive oil
1 cup fresh-grated parmesan and Romano
cheeses, mixed together
½ cup crumbled gorgonzola cheese
2 Jersey tomatoes, quartered and cut in half, or
grape tomatoes
Fresh-ground black pepper
Fresh parsley, chopped for garnish
Salt and pepper to taste

In a medium sauté pan, place ¼ cup olive oil and sauté garlic cloves (do not brown). Add fresh parsley, basil, salt, and pepper. Cook for about 2 minutes. Add the canned tomatoes. Let simmer on low heat for 20–25 minutes. When pasta is cooked, drain well, reserving some of the pasta water. Place in serving bowl and toss while still hot with a good handful of grated cheese. Toss well but lightly. Now, add the pesto and toss lightly again. Add the cooked tomatoes. Add some of the pasta water just to moisten if needed. Add the gorgon-zola cheese and toss. Add the remainder of the grated cheeses. Add a few twists of black pepper. Garnish with tomatoes and fresh-chopped parsley.

DESSERTS

Now, this is where I shine. I love desserts, and I love baking. I enjoy creating fabulous-looking, mouth-watering, tempting desserts. My grandmother was a terrific baker. Her cakes, pies, pastries, and cookies were second to none. They were the biggest layer cakes I ever saw. The aroma of her pies filled the entire block. And, watching her make cookies and creampuffs was a real treat because I always got to lick the bowl. My aunt was also a great baker. She baked every day. Her chocolate chip cookies are the best. Every year for Christmas I make her ricotta and rice cheesecake. I have included my favorites and simplified some recipes, while others I left as they were. Most recipes are rather easy and certainly not time-consuming, but every dessert is deliciously mouthwatering and will bring rave reviews.

Aunt Marie's Chocolate Chips

My Aunt Marie makes the best chocolate chip cookies. They are big, soft, and chewy. Walnuts add that perfect touch that transforms these cookies into "adult" cookies. Several years ago I brought a plate of these cookies into the office and announced, "These are Aunt Marie's chocolate chip cookies." Everyone eagerly took a cookie and after one bite they were asking me where I purchased "Aunt Marie's chocolate chip cookies." I explained that *my* Aunt Marie had *made* them. Aunt Marie was catapulted into cookie stardom and became our official cookie maker. I, on the other hand, never achieved that title. I just could not get the hang of cookie making unless it was in the form of bar cookies, but these chocolate chip cookies I have mastered. Instead of dropping by spoonfuls, try using a small ice cream scoop. You can eliminate the walnuts or add your own little something extra, such as peanut butter chips or white chocolate chips and macadamias. Any way you make them, they are the best!

2¼ cups all-purpose flour
1 teaspoon baking soda
½ teaspoon salt
2 sticks sweet butter, softened
1 cup light brown sugar
⅓ cup fructose
1½ teaspoon vanilla
2 large eggs
12 ounce package mini chocolate morsels
8 ounces chopped walnuts

Preheat over to 350 degrees. Combine flour, baking soda, and salt in small bowl. Set aside. Beat butter, brown sugar, fructose, and vanilla with electric mixer on medium speed until fluffy. Beat in eggs, one at a time, until well blended. With mixer on low speed, gradually add flour mixture and beat until well blended. With wooden spoon or rubber spatula, stir in chocolate morsels and nuts. Scoop by heaping tablespoons and place 2 inches apart on ungreased cookie sheets. Bake for 12–15 minutes or until golden brown. Do not overbake. Let stand about 2 minutes, remove to wire racks to cool. Makes about 36 cookies 3 inches in diameter.

Chocolate Frangelico Layer Cake

The inspiration for this cake came from a TV cooking show I was watching one Saturday afternoon. Two men made a chocolate layer cake that they were brushing with rum, but they returned each layer to the originl baking pan so the layers stayed straight. Usually my layers lean to one side, and for that reason I have avoided making thin layers. Not anymore! Once I saw them place the layers back in the pan, I was so thrilled at the technique, I literally jumped into the kitchen and created this fabulous dessert. The Frangelico gives it a nutty taste of hazelnuts, and of course the chocolate makes it almost sinful. Try it with a dollup of sweetened whipped cream and berries doused with a little Frangelico. You must try it.

Chocolate cake:
1 7 or 8-inch springform pan for baking cake
1 springform pan slightly larger
1 box chocolate fudge cake mix
2 or 3 cups Frangelico Liquor (You may need more.)

Chocolate mousse filling:
16 ounces semi-sweet chocolate
2 eggs
4 egg yolks
2 cups whipping cream
6 tablespoons powdered sugar
4 egg whites
6 tablespoons Frangelico Liquor

Make cake according to package directions replacing liquid with Frangelico liquor. While cake is baking, prepare mousse filling. Melt chocolate until smooth. Let cool to lukewarm, about 10 minutes. Add whole egg and mix well. Add egg yolks and mix until thoroughly blended. Set aside.

When cake has finished baking, allow to cool completely for easy handling. With either electric knife or a very long sharp knife, slice cake into four layers. Place the first layer back on its original baking pan bottom or place it in the larger pan (pan should be only slightly larger than the cake layers). Place the other three layers on either wax paper or parchment. Brush the first layer generously with the Frangelico. Spoon the mousse generously onto the cake. Now, place the second layer onto the mousse, pressing gently and evenly. Brush this layer with Frangelico and spoon mousse onto cake layer. Repeat the process for the third layer, then place the fourth layer on top, pressing gently and evenly, and brush generously with liquor. Place cake in refrigerator for approximately 2 hours or more to allow mousse to set. Cover remaining mousse with plastic wrap, set aside.

Frost and Garnish Cake:

Melt 6 ounces of semi-sweet chocolate. Pour the melted chocolate in a squeeze bottle for chocolate bark or shavings, or spread evenly on a chilled metal surface, such as the bottom of a chilled baking pan. Squeeze chocolate in long thin lines or spread evenly as thin as possible. To make swirls, allow drying slightly, but it should still have a shiny surface. With the end of a metal spatula working away from you, apply pressure in a downward sliding motion, allowing chocolate to curl on the spatula. Gently remove curls or shavings and place on wax paper. You may make the curls as large or as small as you prefer. Remove the chocolate lines with a thin spatula. Refrigerate if not using immediately. When cake is completely cooled and mousse is set, remove from refrigerator, remove sides of pan; do not remove from bottom tray. With flat knife or frosting knife, place mousse on sides of cake, spreading evenly and smoothly and then on top, spreading evenly and smoothly. Take a handful of chocolate jimmies or finely chopped walnuts and press them against side of cake, going all the way around. Repeat as necessary to cover side completely. This may take quite a bit of jimmies, so make sure you have plenty. Take curls and/or shavings, placing on top of cake. Be generous; it will look gorgeous! Garnish cake plate with sweetened berries to which a little Frangelico has been added.

Chocolate Mousse Cake

This rich chocolate dessert has become the all-time favorite with everyone! I have been making this dessert for twenty years, and it never falls short on gasps of excitement when served. The presentation and taste far outshine all other desserts. The first time I made it, I did not have a food processor, and therefore I tried to crush the chocolate wafers with a rolling pin. I thought I had done a good job, but the crumbs were not fine enough and remained hard. I could not cut through the crust. My mother went into the kitchen and brought out a serrated knife, but that only made a mess. We actually served the mousse by spooning it into dessert cups. The mousse tasted fabulous. It took several attempts after that to get the knack of turning those chocolate wafers into a chocolate crust. But I finally mastered it—a food processor. Today I use chocolate-filled chocolate cookies for the crust, together with a food processor. Perfect crust every time! This chocolate mousse cake is my specialty and crowning glory.

Crust:
3 cups chocolate crumbs
½ stick butter, melted

Filling:
1 pound semi-sweet chocolate
2 whole eggs
4 egg yolks
4 egg whites
1 pint heavy cream
6 tablespoons confectioner's sugar

Place chocolate wafers or cookies into food processor and process into very fine crumbs. Measure out 3 cups of crumbs, place in medium bowl, add melted butter, and stir well to moisten. If crumbs appear too dry, melt an additional 1–2 tablespoons, add to crumbs. Press on bottom and up sides of a 9 or 10-inch springform pan. Place in freezer.

Place chocolate in large bowl and microwave 1 minute. Stir and repeat process until all the chocolate is melted and very smooth. Allow to cool 3–4 minutes. Add whole eggs, stirring vigorously making sure eggs are completely incorporated. Add yolks, stirring well, making sure yolks are fully incorporated. Set aside.

In a medium bowl of an electric mixer, whip egg whites on high until stiff peaks form, wiping down sides of bowl with spatula. Set aside. In a large bowl of the electric mixer, whip heavy cream on high until firm, adding powdered sugar 1 tablespoon at a time, continuously wiping down sides with spatula.

With your spatula, add a heaping amount of cream to the chocolate and start folding in. Now, fold in egg whites, a little at a time. Repeat this process until all of the cream and whites have been folded into the chocolate mixture.

Remove the pan from the freezer. Pour the chocolate mixture into the prepared pan, smoothing the top. Place in the refrigerator at least 6 hours or overnight.

To remove from pan, gently slide a thin knife between crust and pan, going all around to loosen, then open pan and gently lift off side of pan. Cake remains on the bottom tin. Place on a dessert dish and decorate with either chocolate swirls or shavings. Add a dollop of whipped cream to each serving. It is completely irresistible.

Chocolate Orange Budino

Budino means pudding in Italian. My grandmother made chocolate budino for several recipes, one of which was chocolate pudding served in pretty individual dessert glass bowls. My other favorites for this pudding are my grandmother's chocolate cream pie, which is second to none, and a longtime old standby favorite, icebox cake. She always used evaporated milk and cooked the pudding. My recipe is slightly different. In fact, there is no cooking. A child could make this pudding, and it would turn out perfect. And, staying true to form, I have reduced the calories by eliminating most of the sugar and fat. I prefer to use fat-free evaporated milk because it gives the pudding a rich texture. Orange cream flavoring does not add any calories but gives a delicious hint of orange together with a sprinkling of orange zest seasoning.

2 boxes fat-free and sugar free instant chocolate fudge pudding mix
2 cans chilled fat-free evaporated milk
2 ounces cold water
3 caps orange cream flavoring

Orange zest seasoning
Whipped topping
Slices of fresh orange for each serving

Place all ingredients in mixing bowl. Beat with wire whisk until thickened, about 1 minute. Pour into dessert bowls, sprinkle with just a little more orange zest. Refrigerate approximately 20 minutes. Serve with a dollop of whipped topping. Add an orange slice for garnish. Scrumptious!

Grandmom's Tomato Soup Cake

My grandmother made this cake; in fact, I believe I can go so far as to say this was her original creation. No one had ever heard of tomato soup cake before, but locating her recipe has been an ongoing search. Neither my mother or I ever had the recipe; therefore recreating this cake has also been an ongoing effort. After many attempts over the years, I do believe I have attained the same great taste and texture. This cake may be served with powdered sugar sprinkled on top or, my favorite, chocolate icing. Either way, you can't go wrong.

    16 ounces canned tomato soup
    1 cup oil
    3 cups sugar
    4 eggs, beaten
    ⅔ cups water
    3½ cups flour
    1 teaspoon baking powder

2 teaspoons baking soda
2 teaspoons salt
½ teaspoon cloves
1 teaspoon cinnamon
1 teaspoon allspice
1 teaspoon nutmeg

In a large bowl of an electric mixer combine tomato soup, oil, sugar, and eggs at medium speed. Add remaining ingredients and continue mixing. Pour into a greased 10 cup tube pan (I prefer to use an angel food pan). Bake for 1 hour at 350 degrees or until knife inserted in center comes out clean. Remove from oven and let stand for 10–15 minutes. Remove from pan and cool completely. Sprinkle with powdered sugar or drizzle chocolate icing.

Harvey Wallbanger Cake

Talk about a throwback to the 70s, here it is. I made this cake in the early 70s after purchasing a bottle of Galliano Liqueur for the holidays. On the neck of the bottle was tied a small booklet with recipes. This was one that I tried. I tell a cute story about my daughter, Sherrie, who was about three or four years old at the time. Whenever I baked, she waited to lick the bowl and beaters from the electric mixer. Since this recipe called for vodka and Galliano, I told her she could not. After I had finished icing the cake, I left it on the counter in the kitchen and I went to my room to change clothes. When I walked back into the kitchen, I let out a gasp! Every bit of icing had been licked off the cake. When Sherrie heard me, she came running into the kitchen and announced, *in a very loud voice*, "That was good, Mommy, better make more." The cake was a true hit and when I find something I like that everyone else enjoys also, I stick with it. Like my cheesecake and chocolate mousse cakes, which I have been making for almost three decades, I have been making this recipe for over thirty-three years. A good idea might be to make two Harvey Wallbangers—one for the cake, and one for yourself. Sherrie would agree.

Cake:
1 box orange cake mix
1 box instant vanilla pudding
¼ cup oil
4 eggs
1 Harvey Wallbanger (recipe to follow)

Drizzle:
1 cup powdered sugar
½ teaspoon vodka
½ teaspoon orange juice
½ teaspoon Galliano

Harvey Wallbanger:
In a tall glass add ¾ cup orange juice, ¼ cup vodka, ¼ cup Galliano (stirred not shaken).

For the cake, mix all ingredients together and just one of the Harvey Wallbangers. Grease and flour a bundt pan. Bake at 350 degrees for 45–55 minutes, or until thin knife inserted in center comes out clean. Cool cake in pan about 15 minutes. Remove from pan and allow to cool completely. Drizzle icing over top and down sides. Serve with a few orange twists as garnish.

Tips:
- If the cake mix has pudding in the mix, do not add the box of pudding.
- Spray baking pan with non-stick cooking spray before greasing.
- You may want to make a second batch of icing for extra drizzle.

Icebox Cake

I believe this is truly a traditional Neapolitan Italian-American dessert. What I remember so fondly was that after my grandmother made her "Icebox Cake," my big treat was licking the pudding pot. This delicious dessert was made with graham crackers and her chocolate pudding. Today, I still use the graham crackers, but for a different texture, I use the chocolate-covered graham cookies, or you can use chocolate graham crackers. If you want the traditional method, use regular graham crackers. Either one works well. Follow the recipe for chocolate orange budino. If you wish, you can eliminate the orange flavoring or leave it. Either way it is delicious and certainly chocolate. I like to serve it with sweetened fresh berries on the side—looks pretty and tastes great.

Chocolate budino recipe, doubled
1 box graham crackers or 1 package chocolate covered graham cookies

Allow pudding to set 2–3 minutes to thicken before assembling cake. On a large flat serving plate, line graham crackers side by side, 4 across. Place heaping spoonfuls of pudding on crackers, spreading to ends. Repeat for 6 layers of graham crackers, spooning pudding on to each layer. Finish with pudding on top. Refrigerate about 1 hour to chill and soften graham crackers.

Joyce Ann's Cheesecake

And that is exactly what everyone calls this cheesecake. The recipe for this delicious cheesecake was given to me by a patron of my family's restaurant, Covino's, on Father's Day, 1972 or 1973. The restaurant had taken reservations for "Sunday Dinner with Dad." One of the patrons, who called to make a reservation for Father's Day, asked if she could bring her own dessert. Of course it was okay. When she arrived, she handed the cheesecake to my mother and asked that it be refrigerated. My mother, who salivates at the mention of desserts, asked what it was. When the patron replied homemade cheesecake, my mother told her in no uncertain terms that a piece must be saved for her. The cheesecake was served and a piece delivered to my mother, and my mother walked over to me and said, "Get this recipe." Well, of course I did, and I have been making it ever since. In fact, it has become my signature piece. I have revised the original recipe by using light cream cheese and light sour cream. I also use 1 tablespoon of vanilla in place of the original amount of 1½ teaspoons, and I add 1 cup of finely ground walnuts to the crust. I bake it at 300 degrees with a water bath instead of the original 350 degrees and no water bath. I've made these changes over many years of experimenting and I have found this method to work out best, and you can't beat the flavor. Everyone will rave and go back for seconds; remember, it's light.

2 cups graham cracker crumbs
1 stick butter, melted
½ cup sugar
1 cup finely ground walnuts
3 8-ounce packages light cream cheese, room temperature
1 cup sugar
5 eggs
1½ pints light sour cream
1 tablespoon vanilla extract
1 can cherry pie filling for garnish

Preheat oven to 300 degrees. Place crumbs, melted butter, sugar, and nuts in medium-sized bowl. With a fork, stir all ingredients to mix well. Press firmly into bottom of a 9-inch springform pan. Place pan in freezer. With electric mixer, beat cream cheese and sugar until light and fluffy. Add eggs, one at a time, mixing well after each addition. Fold in the sour cream and vanilla. Remove pan from freezer. Pour batter into prepared pan and place on baking sheet with a medium-sized bowl of water. Bake for 1 hour. Turn off oven but do not remove. Cheesecake should remain in oven until cool enough to handle; this should eliminate cracking. When cheesecake is removed from the oven, place in refrigerator and allow to cool completely. Garnish with the cherry pie filling by making three rows of cherries around the top of the cake. Serve chilled with a dollop of sweetened whipped cream.

Lemon Chiffon Dessert

The credit for this recipe goes to my Aunt Marie. Although originally made as a pie, I figured it would make a fabulous chiffon mousse. So, that is exactly what I did. Serve this in a very pretty glass bowl. The bright yellow color of this dessert is inviting by itself. But, I like to mound dollops of fresh-whipped cream on top and drizzle chocolate syrup over the cream. You will not believe how fabulous lemon and chocolate taste together. Let your guests help themselves, and watch them go back for seconds.

2 packages unflavored gelatin
1 cup cold water
8 egg yolks
1 cup sugar
⅔ cup fresh lemon juice from 6 lemons
Lemon zest from 2 lemons
8 egg whites
1 cup sugar
1 cup heavy cream for whipping

2 caps full of vanilla
4 tablespoons powdered sugar

Dissolve gelatin in water. Set aside. In top of double boiler, place yolks, sugar, lemon juice, and zest. With wire whisk, stir constantly until thick, about 10–15 minutes. Remove from heat, set aside. Beat egg whites. Gradually add sugar. Continue beating until stiff peaks form. With a rubber spatula, fold whites into yolk mixture until thoroughly incorporated. Pour into serving bowl and refrigerate at least 6 hours or overnight. Before serving, whip 1 cup of heavy cream. Add 2 caps of vanilla and 4 tablespoons of powdered sugar. Continue whipping until stiff. Mound cream decoratively on top of dessert. Drizzle chocolate syrup over cream. Serve very cold.

Pizza-gaina Bread

Meat and cheese filled dessert bread

How delicious is delicious? *This* is delicious! First, let me say, I haven't the slightest idea how to spell this. I am sure the pronunciation was a little broken-English, together with a Naples dialect and hence *pizza-gaina*. Regardless of what it's called, this tasty treat is so fabulous that each bite fills your mouth with the savory flavors from the meats and cheeses, while the bread has a slightly sweet taste. My grandmother served pizza-gaina cold as dessert bread with coffee or *demi-tasse*. It was always an Easter treat. However, I make it for both Easter and Christmas and just about anytime in between. I believe in making life simple, so I buy store-bought frozen pizza dough instead of making my own. Believe me, no one will know. When I told my mother I used frozen pizza dough from the supermarket, she was very surprised. She said, "How ingenious and so delicious." I was thrilled. This recipe calls for a 9x13 heavy baking pan. I use an old restaurant pan because it is heavy stainless steel.

2 frozen pizza dough balls

½ pound each sliced pepperoni, Genoa salami,
and sweet cappicolla

4 ounces mozzarella, cut into small cubes

32 ounces Ricotta

8 eggs

Dash of salt and pepper

Olive oil

Cooking spray

1 beaten egg for brushing the dough

Place ricotta in a very large mixing bowl. In another bowl, beat the eggs, then add to the ricotta. Chop meats into small pieces. Add to mixture. Add cubed mozzarella and a dash of salt and pepper. Set aside. Spray baking pan well with cooking spray. Take your pizza dough and knead it slightly. Stretch to fit on bottom and up the sides and just over the top of the pan. Pour the ricotta mixture into the dough in pan. Take your second round of dough, knead slightly and stretch as though you are making pizza. Place on top of the ricotta mixture and to the end of the pan. Take the dough that is slightly over the edge of the pan and just fold in on top of the second piece of dough, making a decorative edge. Brush with beaten egg to give the bread a glossy crust when browning. Place in 350 degree oven and bake for 1½ hours, turning pan 180 degrees every ½ hour to ensure even browning. Continue baking until there is no liquid in center. Crust should be golden brown and shiny. Allow cooling for 10–15 minutes. Remove from pan by turning upside down onto a kitchen towel placed on a flat surface. Let cool completely before cutting. Refrigerate wrapped in foil.

Rice and Ricotta Cake

My Aunt Marie gave me this recipe after she made it, and of course, brought some to my mother. My mother loved it, and therefore I *had* to have the recipe. This is a ricotta cheese cake that could not be easier. It makes a fairly large cake, which freezes well. When I prepare this ricotta cheese cake for the Christmas holidays, I add green maraschino cherries along with the red. You will need a 17 x 12 x 2½ baking pan.

1 dozen large eggs, beaten
1 cup sugar
1 teaspoon vanilla
1 cup cooked rice
3 pounds Ricotta cheese
1 small bottle maraschino cherries without stems, drained and sliced
1 handful chocolate bits
1 box yellow cake mix

Preheat oven to 350 degrees. Prepare rice and set aside. Mix cake according to package directions. Set aside. In large bowl whisk together the eggs, sugar, and vanilla. Pour the ricotta and rice into the egg mixture. Set aside. Pour the prepared yellow cake mixture into a greased and floured pan. Pour ricotta mixture on top, do not mix together. Sprinkle with chopped cherries and chocolate bits. Bake approximately 1 hour. Cake is done when sharp knife inserted into center comes out clean. Allow to cool completely. Sprinkle with confectioner's sugar. Cut into 1-inch squares.

Hint: You could cook the rice using this easy-to-follow table:

1 cup raw rice = 3 cups cooked. Or, do as I do, buy the rice already cooked. You can find it on the shelf in your local grocery store.

INDEX

D

E

F